BRITISH RAILWAYS LOCOMOTIVES

THE FIRST 12 YEARS (1948–60)

Barry P. Hoper

ISBN 1–872768–15–6

Copyright 1997 Barry Hoper and S.C.T. Publishing

Published by S.C.T. Publishing, 3, Morley Drive, Bishop's Waltham, Hampshire SO32 1RX

Printed and bound in Great Britain by Bookcraft (Bath) Ltd, Midsomer Norton, Somerset

(Above) What a magnificent sight Gresley A3 4-6-2 No 60089 'Felstead', in lined blue, makes as she departs from Edinburgh Waverley with the 1.25pm train to Carlisle on 24 March 1951. *Photo: J Robertson.*

(Front cover) 'Princess Coronation' class 4-6-2 No 46223 'Princess Alice' awaits departure from Glasgow Central with the 'Royal Scot' on 9 June 1956. 46223 was originally built in June 1937 as a streamlined locomotive, the casing being removed in August 1946, and the engine was finally withdrawn from service in October 1963 from Glasgow (Polmadie) shed. *Photo: J Robertson.*

CONTENTS

INTRODUCTION

My own interest in railways started in my pre-school years but my first recollection was sitting on the crossing gate by the sewage works, just to the south of Creekmoor Halt between Poole and Broadstone. This location was hardly a Mecca for trainspotters but I delighted in the rural atmosphere of the line which, at that time, boasted mainly of Drummond M7 tanks and Class 700 locomotives on the services to Brockenhurst and Salisbury. However, the Somerset and Dorset Railway also ran over these former LSWR metals to the terminus at Bournemouth West and these trains were pulled by a variety of locomotive classes which included 9Fs, Bulleid Pacifics, 7Fs 4Fs 2Ps, 8Fs and the odd surprise. Although I later aspired to become a 'trainspotter' and frequented busier rail centres such as Bournemouth Central, Bristol, Swindon and Doncaster, my love of the 'Castleman's Corkscrew', the line from Poole to Brockenhurst via Ringwood has never left me. As I write this preface, Southern Railway enamel station signs, known as targets, from Poole, Creekmoor Halt, Broadstone, Wimborne and Fordingbridge keep sentinel on the walls of my study.

My affair with the darkroom started briefly after I joined the Royal Air Force in 1966. At RAF Cosford where I served my apprenticeship in Telegraphy, I learned the basic skills of photographic printing through the good offices of the Station's Photographic Club. My lasting memory of the prints that I produced at that time was dust. Those were the days of the condenser enlarger which managed to detect the smallest piece of dust and magnify it to tree-trunk proportions. Little did I realise in 1966 that it would be 30 years before I renewed my acquaintance with the darkroom. It was in fact December 1996 when a friend, Keith Jones, decided that I was to become the custodian of his collection of railway negatives. This was the start of the labour of love that now seems to consume most of my leisure time. However, the significant event which has brought about the publishing of this book happened in the Summer of 1997 when another old friend, Ron White, of Colour-Rail fame, passed me the negative collection of John Robertson. It had always been Ron's intention to publish a book of John Robertson's photographs but, unfortunately, Colour-Rail demands 25-hours a day of Ron's time and therefore that duty has fallen to me.

In addition to his own work, the negatives in the former John Robertson collection were taken by his old friends, William Hermiston and A G Ellis and augmented by photographs from the cameras of J A Whaley, A W Croughton and J T Rutherford, C L Kerr inter alia. However, this book celebrates the work of John Robertson, Willy Hermiston and George Ellis who, as well as all being extremely skilled photographers, were also the best of chums, travelling the length and breadth of the country

to record our railway heritage for us to enjoy today and for generations to come. So, who are these men?

John Robertson was born in 1908 on the border of Edinburgh and Leith. He was one of three children, having a brother and a sister. His father was a metal-worker and John became an instrument technician. With John's interest in woodwork and railways, it was inevitable that this early enthusiasm was for model railways. However, in 1945, when photographic materials were still scarce, John began to experiment with railway photography, a hobby which was to last until 1974. His first camera used $\frac{1}{4}$ glass plates. John would carry two-dozen of these plates on a day trip, as well as the camera, tripod and sustenance! But John wanted to get closer to the action and applied to Haymarket for an all-line photographic permit. However, before the railways would issue such a permit, it was incumbent on a railway official to assess the standard of John's photography. After satisfying the inspecting official, John obtained his permit and soon became a regular visitor to Haymarket shed where he would provide footplate crews with photographs of themselves with their charges. John retired in 1973 and finished photographing railways in 1974 after a visit to Australia and New Zealand. John now lives in Leith in a retirement flat which stands on the former trackbed outside the old Leith Central, a haunt frequently photographed by John in the 1950s. As well as black and white photography, John also took many colour transparencies which are available through Colour-Rail.

Willy Hermiston lived in Edinburgh and earned his living as a Funeral Director. Willy started his railway photography before the war but joined forces with John Robertson in 1945. The two men became good friends and travelled extensively to photograph the railway scene. Indeed, on some negatives taken by Willy, it is possible to see John in action with his camera and vice versa; one such example is included in this book. On Willy's death in 1970, John Robertson inherited Willy's negative collection which also included work by A W Croughton, J T Rutherford, C L Kerr, and J A Whaley.

At the time these photographs were taken, George Ellis lived in Glasgow. He and John Robertson had an agreement that, whenever possible, they would each take 2 photographs of each railway subject and give each other the spare negative.

Finally, I am grateful for the assistance given to me by Ron White, Dick Whittington, Mike Rose and Stu Robinson. I must also thank Peter Ifold without whose enthusiasm this book would never have been published. Finally, to my dear wife Janet, for putting up with those lonely hours while I sweated it out in the darkroom to produce the photographs.

BIBLIOGRAPHY

What Happened to Steam, P B Hands.
Passengers No More, G Daniels & L A Dench.
Locomotives of the LNER, RCTS.
The Standard Steam Locomotives of British Railways, R P Bradley.
Railway Observer, RCTS.
Locomotives at the Grouping, Casserley & Johnston.
LMS Engines, J W P Rowledge.

TO MY SON JAMIE WHO WAS BORN ON 11 APRIL 1997

Barry P. Hoper

(Above) John Robertson's first photograph of the day at Totnes on 1 August 1955 was of 14xx 0-4-2T No 1470 leaving on a local service to Ashburton. The locomotive is unusually in lined black. The carriage-destination board 'Totnes' is still in place on the auto-coach.

(Above) Enthusiasts on a shed bash to Bristol on Sunday 8 August 1954 are watched by the fireman who is watering his charge, a Swindon 57xx Pannier Tank No 3645. The fireman obviously had time to spare otherwise he would have surely opened the lid of the opposite tank to allow the displaced air to escape and thereby fill the tanks quicker. The locomotive remained at Swindon until withdrawn in May 1962. *Photo: J Robertson.*

(Above)   During his summer holiday to the West Country in 1955, John Robertson photographed 54xx 0-6-0PT No 5403 at Taunton on 8 August with a local service to Westbury. The locomotive still sported its GWR origins on the tender. The backing arm on the platform-mounted bracket signal is a particular gem. After his day at Taunton, John moved on to Bristol Temple Meads and spent the 10 August at Swindon.

(Above)   0-6-0PT No 3794 is seen on station pilot duty at Exeter St Davids on 7 August 1954. Note the slaking pipe hanging from the cab. 3794 remained at Exeter until transfer to Oxford in October 1963, finally being withdrawn in December 1964.   *Photo: J Robertson.*

(Above) 28xx Collett class 2-8-0 No 2899 hurries along the Devon coast between Dawlish and Teignmouth with a mixed freight on a glorious summer's day in 1959. The Collett locomotives numbered 2884-99 and 3800-66 were introduced in 1938 with side-window cab. Although usually a Southall engine, No 2899 spent nearly 3 years at Plymouth (Laira) between 1959 and 1961.   *Photo: W Hermiston.*

(Above) Hall class 4-6-0 No 6913 'Levens Hall' coasts into Penzance on 4 August 1954 with 'The Cornishman'. The Cornishman ran from Wolverhampton to Penzance via Stratford, Cheltenham, Bristol and Plymouth and was instituted when BR(W) introduced a policy to name second division trains. The leg from Plymouth was a Laira turn and hence the appearance of Laira engine 6913.   *Photo: J Robertson.*

7

(Above) Modified Hall No 7905 'Fowey Hall' and 49xx No 5967 'Bickmarsh Hall' take the centre road through Totnes on 1 August 1955. In the siding to the left can be seen a flat wagon with the predecessor to today's container traffic, For a small amount of money, the railway would collect items for conveyance door-to-door or 'to be called for' from the nearest railway station. *Photo: W Hermiston*

(Above) 'Manor' 78xx class 4-6-0 No 7820 'Dinmore Manor' and 'Hall' 49xx class 4-6-0 No 5901 'Hazel Hall' take the through road at Totnes on 1 August 1955. The milk sidings in the background led into the Up platform which enabled wagons to be easily added to Up trains. *Photo: W Hermiston*

(Above)   Hall class 4-6-0s Nos 6936 'Breccles Hall' and 6940 'Didlington Hall' enter Totnes on an up express on 1 August 1955. The road bridge in the background is being rebuilt and also worthy of note is the off-set signal post, behind the telegraph pole on the left, which gave visibility of the semaphore to approaching trains. *Photo: J Robertson.*

(Below)   'Castle' 4073 class 4-6-0 No 5064 'Bishop's Castle' waits at Teignmouth with the 11.10am Penzance to Wolverhampton on 2 August 1955. An extremely successful design which was still being produced by British Railways as the first of GWR members were being withdrawn from service. They shared responsibility with the 'Kings' for the crack expresses such as the 'Inter City', 'Cornish Riviera' and 'The Bristolian'. *Photo: W Hermiston.*

(*Left*) Castle class 4-6-0 No 7004 'Eastnor Castle' passes Teignmouth on 4 August 1954 with the Torbay Express which was routed from Kingswear to Paddington. The locomotive was fitted with a double chimney in February 1958.

Photo: J Robertson.

(Above)   49xx 4-6-0 No 5925 'Eastcote Hall' and Castle class 4-6-0 No 5021 'Whittington Castle' head through Totnes on 1 August 1955 while 14xx 0-4-2T No 1470 waits in the platform with the Ashburton branch train. Trains were always piloted westwards from Newton Abbot to Plymouth to assist the climbs up Dainton (1 in 36) and Rattery.   *Photo: J Robertson.*

(Below)   4-6-0 'Hall' 49xx class No 4948 'Northwick Hall' pilots 'King' class 4-6-0 No 6026 'King John' on a train at Shaldon Bridge on 4 August 1955. Shaldon bridge carried the road from Shaldon to Teignmouth.   *Photo: W Hermiston.*

(*Above*) 'King' class 4-6-0 No 6008 'King James II' on The Cornish Riviera at Teignmouth on 4 August 1959. The 'King' class were the most powerful 4-6-0 locomotives ever to work in Britain and they were the mainstay of the Western Region premier expresses from 1927 until the Summer of 1962. The nameplates from the class are the most sought after memento for railwayana collectors with plates changing hands for around £20,000. 6008 was withdrawn from Wolverhampton in July 1957. *Photo: W Hermiston.*

(Above) 51xx class 2-6-2T No 5195 stands in Newton Abbot on 16 August 1957. The young lad stood on the platform is unsure what to make of this noisy machine and chooses to keep his hands firmly clamped over his ears. The hut on the platform was used for locomotive crews to muster. *Photo: J Robertson.*

(Above) 'Castle' class 4-6-0 No 4096 'Highclere Castle' waits at Newton Abbot on 16 August 1957 alongside 'King' class 4-6-0 No 6025 'King Henry III' which is on 'The Mayflower' (8.30am Plymouth to Paddington). *Photo: W Hermiston.*

(*Above*) 'Grange' 68xx class 4-6-0 No 6827 'Llanfrechfa Grange' heads the 8.10am Manchester (London Road) to Penzance at Exeter St Davids on 6 August 1955. No 6827 carried an extended 'nameplate and was photographed in plain black livery. The ladder on the walkway above the station awning was used to gain access to the roof and note also the smoke deflectors on the signal gantry.
Photo: W Hermiston.

(Above) 49xx class 4-6-0 No 6940 'Didlington Hall' in lined black at Exeter St Davids with the 7.0am Plymouth to Paddington on 2 August 1955. The locomotive is fitted with a Hawksworth flat-sided tender. *Photograph: W Hermiston.*

(Below) 'Castle' 4073 class 4-6-0 No 5003 'Lulworth Castle' drifts past Exeter Riverside Signal Box into Exeter St Davids with the 8.55am Wolverhampton to Penzance on 16 August 1957. A southern banker waits in the holding siding. *Photo: W Hermiston.*

(Above) 'County' 10xx class 4-6-0 No 1018 'County of Leicester' in lined black waits for the road at Exeter St Davids with the 8.0am Kingswear to Paddington on 6 August 1955.   *Photo: W Hermiston.*

(Below) 47xx 2-8-0 heavy freight locomotive No 4708 simmers at Exeter St Davids while it waits for the road with the 1.28pm Paddington to Kingswear on 6 August 1955. These heavy freight locomotives were often pressed into passenger service on summer Saturdays.   *Photo: W Hermiston.*

(*Above*)   'King' class 4-6-0 No 6012 'King Edward VI' in lined blue livery at Exeter St Davids with the Up 'Mayflower' (8.30am Plymouth to Paddington) in the early 1950s. Note the 'LA' GWR style shed code for Plymouth (Laira) applied behind the buffer beam. The last 'King' to retain the blue livery was 6014 'King Henry VII'. *Photo: W Hermiston.*

(*Below*)   57xx class 0-6-0PT No 9765 retaining its GWR livery shunts coal wagons at Exeter on 7 August 1954. At least 2 other sister engines can be seen in the picture including No 5760. 9765 remained at Exeter until withdrawal in December 1961 while 5760 succumbed to her fate in October 1957. *Photo: J Robertson.*

(Above) King class 4-6-0 No 6023 'King Edward II' enters Exeter St Davids on 7 August 1954 with the 11.50am Penzance to Paddington, while ex-SR class E1/R 0-6-2T locomotives Nos 32135 and 32124 return from banking duties at Exeter Central. Just behind 'King Edward II's smokebox can be seen Exeter West Signal Box which is now the largest mechanical box in preservation. The area to the left of the picture was South Devon carriage sidings which has now been redeveloped for housing; the calling-on signals gave access to the sidings. *Photo: J Robertson.*

(Below) Star class 4-6-0 No 4061 'Glastonbury Abbey' leaves Exeter St Davids on the 9.10am Wolverhampton to Paignton on 6 August 1955 while an up train headed by Castle class No 5003 'Lulworth Castle' heads into Exeter St Davids. *Photo: J Robertson.*

(Above)   45xx 2-6-2T No 5571 comes off the Minehead branch into Norton Fitzwarren on 8 August 1955. The Barnstaple branch and main line is to the left. The signalling has been simplified by the removal of the crossover and, consequently, the small arm dolly has been removed from the post. Note also the plate indicator for the relief line on the signal in the bottom left corner of the picture.

Photo: J Robertson.

(Below)   49xx Hall class 4-6-0 No 4917 'Crosswood Hall', in lined-black livery, leaves Taunton on a down stopping service on 8 August 1955. Few places on the Western Region had the plethora of lines to be found at Taunton. *Photo: J Robertson.*

(Above) Grange 4-6-0 No 6846 'Ruckley Grange' on its home shed at Bristol St Philip's Marsh on 7 August 1954. The locomotive is fitted with a large tender and has '1.30 Up' chalked on the buffer – its next, or last, duty perhaps? 6846 remained at St Philip's Marsh for her remaining years, except for a final 3 months at Bristol Barrow Road being withdrawn from there September 1964. St Philip's Marsh was the largest engine shed in Bristol and was to be found on the south side of the Bristol avoiding line.   *Photo: J Robertson.*

(Below) 43xx 2-6-0 No 6364 heads an empty stock working going out to Malago Vale on 8 August 1954. The class was designed by Churchward and with their light axle weight were able to work over most of the Western Region and were seen mostly on freight and local passenger services. 6364 eventually finished up at Stourbridge from where withdrawal came in November 1964.   *Photo: J Robertson.*

(Above) 28xx class 2-8-0 heavy freight locomotive No 3819 has a clear road through Swindon with a down freight on 10 August 1955. The carriage works can be seen to the left of the picture. This view was taken on the penultimate day of John Robertson and Willy Hermiston's 1955 summer holiday in the west country. The 12 August found them at Eastleigh before they returned to Edinburgh.

(Below) 72xx class 2-8-2T No 7211 ex-works at Swindon on 10 August 1955 along with 'Castle' class No 5023 'Brecon Castle'. In the preparation shed in the background 'Hall' 49xx class No 5916 'Trinity Hall' waits her turn in the works. *Photo: W Hermiston.*

(Above) 28xx 2-8-0 Collett heavy freight locomotive No 3853 leaves Twyford with a mixed freight from Severn Tunnel Junction on 30 July 1955.
Photo: J Robertson.

(Below) Modified Hall 4-6-0 No 6974 'Bryngwyn Hall' in lined black at Twyford on 30 July 1955 with the 11.35am Paddington to Carmarthen. These locomotives were designed by Hawksworth and introduced in 1944; a development of the 'Hall' class with larger super-heater and the main frames in one piece. 6974 almost survived to the end of Western Region steam being withdrawn from Oxford in May 1965.
Photo: J Robertson.

(Above)   43xx class 2-6-0 No 5396 eases a mixed freight from Cheltenham through Andover Junction in 1955. 5396 was finally withdrawn in May 1960 from Worcester.   *Photo: W Hermiston.*

(Above)   45xx 2-6-2T No 4575, in plain black, stands outside Porthmadoc shed in July 1955 sporting a large lion-over-wheel emblem on the tank side. The engine spent most of its service at Machynlleth before withdrawal in August 1960.   *Photo: A G Ellis.*

(*Above*) 58xx 0-4-2T No 5803 (non-auto fitted) stands at Barmouth on 11 July 1955. The locomotive is in plain black with a small lion-over-wheel on the tank side; the tanks were not large enough to accommodate the larger sized emblem. *Photo: A G Ellis.*

(*Above*) 2251 class 0-6-0 No 3201, fitted with a Dean tender, enters Afon Wen on 10 July 1954. Afon Wen station closed on 7 December 1964; the same day that passenger services were withdrawn on the former London North Western line from Afon Wen to Bangor (Menai Bridge). *Photo: J Robertson.*

(*Below*) 43xx 2-6-0 No 5328 awaiting to depart from Afon Wen on 9 July 1955 with a train for Pwllheli. The assisting engine is BR Standard Class 2 No 78005. The GWR always had a perversion that the main engine should lead the train. *Photo: A G Ellis.*

(Left) A grey autumn day finds 94xx class 0-6-0PT No 8428 resting between duties as station pilot at Birmingham Snow Hill on 2 October 1954; time for the crew to digest the contents of the morning daily. This class of locomotive was unpopular on pilot duties because of poor visibility from the cab. One could not reach the brake handle and see the shunter's signals from the cab at the same time.

Photo: A G Ellis.

(Below) Another view of Birmingham Snow Hill as 43xx class 2-6-0 No 9314 on a down mixed freight waits for the signal at the north end of the station on 2 October 1954. 9314 was withdrawn from Shrewsbury in September 1962.   *Photo: A G Ellis.*

(Above) During John Robertson and Willie Hermiston's summer 1956 holiday to the Southern Region, from the 5th to the 17th August, John captured N15 'King Arthur' class No 30801 'Sir Melio de Logres' passing Abbotscliff signal box on a London Bridge to Dover working on 6 August 1956. The birdcage set dates from 1900 and shows clearly the glazed section above the tender through which the guard could view the road ahead.   *Photo: J Robertson.*

(Above) Unrebuilt 'Merchant Navy' class 4-6-2 No 35025 'Brocklebank Line' in blue livery is turned at Dover in the early 1950s to work a Dover to London Bridge turn. The picture was taken 4 months before the locomotive was rebuilt.   *Photo: W Hermiston.*

27

(Above) AIX class 0-6-0 No 32670 shunts ash wagons at St Leonards shed on 9 August 1956. This locomotive remained at St Leonards until 1957, primarily for use on the former Kent & East Sussex Railway. Although introduced in 1911, this locomotive soldiered on until November 1963 when it was withdrawn from Eastleigh and now enjoys a new lease of life in preservation. *Photo: J Robertson.*

(Above) Class V 'Schools' 4-4-0 No 30904 'Lancing' hurries through Tonbridge with a London Bridge to Folkestone working on 12 August 1956. The 'Schools' were the most powerful 4-4-0 locomotives in the country, boasting 3 cylinders, large heating surfaces and high boiler pressure. Each locomotive bore the name of a famous school in the South of England. John Robertson can be seen at the end of the platform. *Photo: W Hermiston.*

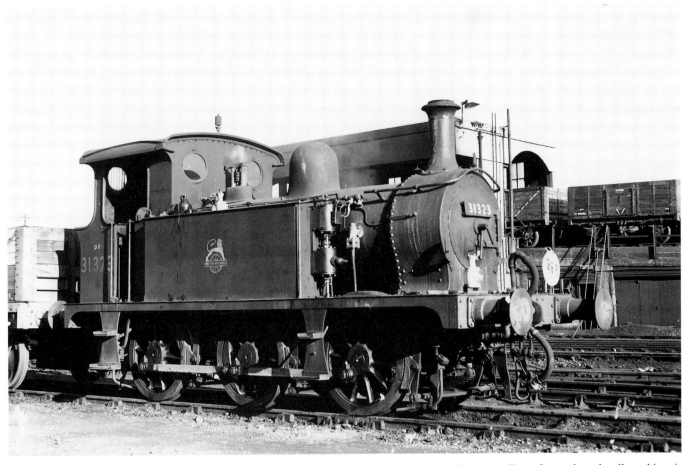

(Above)   Wainwright P class 0-6-0 No 31323 originally designed by the South East and Chatham railway for push-and-pull working, is captured shunting at Dover on 8 August 1956. Shortly afterwards the locomotive was put into store and transferred to Ashford on withdrawal in August 1957 for scrapping.   *Photo: J Robertson.*

(Above)   Class J 0-6-4T No 31595 stands by the coaling stage at Ashford sporting early British Railways livery. This class of 5 engines comprised the last 0-6-4T locomotives in British Railways stock in Great Britain. The engines were designed by Wainwright, and built in 1913 for the South East & Chatham railway for outer-suburban work. 31595 was withdrawn from service in April 1951 and the class was rendered extinct, in September 1951, with the withdrawal of 31595.   *Photo: W Hermiston.*

(*Above*) 'West Country' class 4-6-2 No 34103 'Calstock', heads the Up 'Golden Arrow' past Archcliffe Junction signal box on 4 August 1957. The junction served the lines to Dover Pier and Dover Priory. In this picture taken by Willy Hermiston, John Robertson can be seen strolling towards the signal box.

(Right) Wainwright 'C' class 0-6-0 No 31191, fitted with a Stirling steam reverser, is captured at Dover Priory on 6 August 1957. No fewer than 109 engines of this class were constructed between 1900 and 1908, 31191 being built at Ashford in 1900. One of the class, No 31592, was saved for preservation.

Photo: J Robertson.

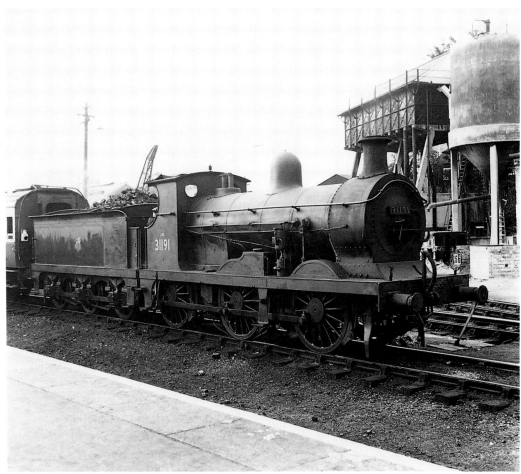

(Above) Class V 'Schools' 4-4-0 No 30931 'King's Wimbledon' runs alongside the cliffs at Abbotscliff on 6 August 1956 with some vintage southern passenger stock. What would John Robertson had thought at the time if he could have known that one of the nameplates off this locomotive would fetch £12,400 at a railwayman auction in 1996? *Photo: J Robertson.*

(Left) Maunsell 'D1' class 4-4-0 No 31545 stands at the back of Longhedge Works, Stewart's Lane on 21 May 1957. The D1s were introduced in 1921 and were rebuilds of classes E and D. The engines were used on passenger workings and were allocated to Ashford, Bricklayers Arms, Faversham, Guildford, Stewarts Lane and Tonbridge. 31545 was withdrawn from Nine Elms in March 1961; the class was extinct by November 1961.

Photo: J Robertson.

(Below) 'D' class 4-4-0 No 31734 at Ashford in 1949. The locomotive's new British Railways' number has been applied in traditional Southern Railway sunshine lettering and a smokebox numberplate has been fitted; however, 'Southern' still remains on the tender. Designed by Wainwright, the 'D's were the first express engines to be built for the South Eastern and Chatham Railway and they were a radical departure from any locomotive which had previously appeared on either of the constituent companies. *Photo: W Hermiston.*

(*Right*) 'R1' class 0-6-0T No 31047 stands in Folkestone Junction shed on 19 May 1957 with sister engine No 31107. The R1s were used for light suburban passenger traffic and were a Wainwright rebuild of the Stirling 'R' class engines. 31047 was to become the last surviving R1, being finally withdrawn from Nine Elms in March 1960.

Photo: J Robertson.

(*Below*)　Maunsell 'L1' class 4-4-0 No 31783 leaves Ramsgate with a Victoria train on 8 August 1956. For use on passenger trains, the L1s were a post-grouping development of the L class with long-travel valves and cab side-window. With the electrification of the Kent Coast, the entire class was transferred to Nine Elms in June 1959 and 31783 was withdrawn from there in November 1961.　*Photo: J Robertson.*

(*Above*) Bulleid 'Q1' class 0-6-0 No 33039 rests on St Leonards shed awaiting its next turn on 9 August 1956. This unconventional class was introduced during the 1939-45 War as an austerity design giving maximum tractive effort with minimum weight per axle and used primarily for heavy freights. 33039 joined 19 others of the class to be withdrawn in 1964. *Photo: J Robertson.*

(Above)   Drummond M7 class 0-4-4T No 30031 in fine condition that belied her 51 years' rests at Feltham in June 1949. This was the first type designed by Dugald Drummond after his appointment to the Locomotive Superintendency in August 1895. The class numbered 105 and, although constructed primarily to cope with the rapidly expanding London suburban traffic, the M7s were to be found all over the Southern Railway's western section.   *Photo: W Hermiston.*

(Below)   Isle of Wight 'O2' class 0-4-4T No W19 'Osborne' is seen in Malachite Green leaving Ryde St Johns in June 1950. W19 was one of the first of 3 locomotives of the class to be withdrawn at Ryde in November 1955; the other 2 engines being W23 'Totland' and W34 'Newport' both ending their service in July of that year. On the Isle of Wight, W24 'Calbourne' and W31 'Chale' soldiered on until March 1967 when the majority of the island's railway network was closed, whilst on the mainland the last 2 survivors were Nos 30199 and 30225 which remained in service until December 1962. In the summer, the signal arms, which gave advanced warning to Cowes and Ventnor trains of Smallbrook Junction, were re-affixed to the signal gantry.   *Photo: Anon.*

(*Above*) Maunsell Z class 0-8-0T No 30954 shunts at Exmouth Junction on 13 August 1954. The class comprised 8 locomotives built at Brighton and designed for working in the principal marshalling sidings. They were employed at Eastleigh, Salisbury, Exmouth Junction and Hither Green. These engines were very powerful and mechanically well suited to their task but they were unpopular with their crews as the extra cylinder and more complicated gearing was rather labour intensive for the rough work on which the engines were employed. *Photo: J Robertson.*

(Above) Ex-London, Brighton, South Coast Railway 'E4' class 0-6-2T No 32510 on duty at Eastleigh on 15 August 1956. The E4s were a development of the earlier E3 class with larger wheels and boiler, together with an extended smokebox. In 1950 a total of 9 E4s were employed at Eastleigh. Worthy of note is the coal-prick attachment bracket on the cab just to the right of the footplate access.

Photo: J Robertson.

(Above) Bulldog Class D15 4-4-0 No 30471 at Eastleigh resplendent in Southern Railway's sunshine lettering. 30471 was eventually cut-up at Eastleigh on 7 August 1954.

Photo: W Hermiston.

(Above)   One of the famous London and South Western Railway 'Greyhound' class No 30284 is seen passing Eastleigh on the through road with an Up stock working from Southampton Terminus on 15 August 1956. *Photo: J Robertson.*

(Above)   Unrebuilt 'Merchant Navy' class No 35020 'Bibby Line' waits on Salisbury shed to take over the Devon Belle at Wilton in 1954. Salisbury shed was re-roofed in 1956. *Photo: W Hermiston.*

(Above)   Ex-London, Brighton & South Coast Railway N-15X 4-6-0 class No 32329 'Stephenson' awaits access to the coaling stage at Eastleigh on 12 August 1955. The signal on the side of the locomotive crew facilities building was the Outdoor Eyesight Test Signal. The individual under test, accompanied by a Footplate Inspector and the Medical Officer, would take up position at a designated point on Campbell Road. To successfully pass the test, the individual had to read correctly the position of the signal which was hand operated from its base.   *Photo: J Robertson.*

(Below)   Also on 12 August 1955, S15 class No 30497 stands at the Eastleigh coaling stage with cylinder drain-cocks open. A Feltham engine, 30497 was eventually withdrawn from there in July 1963.   *Photo: W Hermiston.*

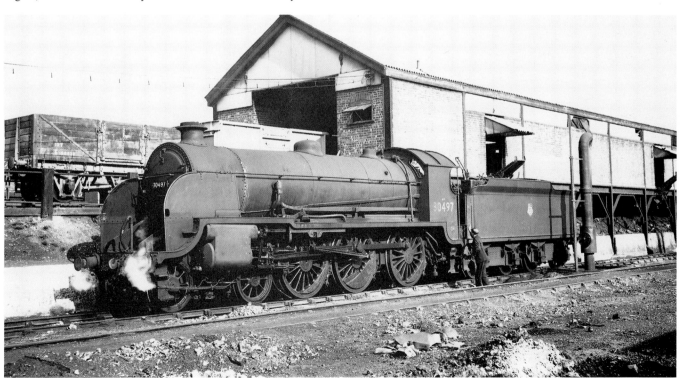

(Above)   Unrebuilt 'Merchant Navy' first of class No 35001 'Channel Packet' prepares to take over the Atlantic Coast Express at Exmouth Junction in 1954. An M7 tank shunts coal wagons in the background. *Photo: W Hermiston.*

(Below)   Maunsell design 'S15' class 4-6-0 No 30846, watched by a look-out man, effortlessly lifts a mixed freight up Honiton Bank with steam to spare on 3 August 1955. 30846 was built at Eastleigh in 1936 and visibly differs from the earlier Urie designed engines of the class by having a straight footplate over the driving-wheels and cylinders, and being fitted with a cab with roof and sides merging in a curve. *Photo: J Robertson.*

(*Left*) Another Maunsell class 'S15' class 4-6-0, this time No 30843 working tender first on a Down engineers' train up Honiton Bank on 3 August 1955. Coach DS1555 was the train's mess van. At the time, engineering work was taking place between Seaton Junction and Honiton Tunnel.

Photo: J Robertson.

(*Left*) 'N' class 2-6-0 No 31844 and 'West Country' No 34104 'Bere Alston' make a noisy start out of Exeter St Davids watched by young train-spotters on 7 August 1954. 'Bere Alston' was only 4 years old when this picture was taken but went on to run 678,853 miles before her withdrawal in the penultimate month of steam on the Southern Region, June 1967. *Photo: J Robertson.*

(Above)   N15 'King Arthur' No 30450 'Sir Kay' at Exmouth Junction shed in 1954. 'Sir Kay' was the shortest nameplate of the class. Note the limescale on the boiler casing from a recent boiler washout. *Photo: W Hermiston.*

(Below)   Adams 0415 class 4-4-2T No 30583 rests at Axminster between duties on the Lyme Regis branch. 30583 was withdrawn in July 1961 but is now preserved on the Bluebell Railway. The Lyme Regis branch fell to the Beeching axe on 19 November 1965. *Photo: W Hermiston.*

(*Above*)   This photograph of class S15 No 30847 lifting a Down local up Honiton Bank near Willmington village was taken by Willie Hermiston on 3 August 1955. In the following photograph of the same train, taken by John Robertson, Willie can be seen snapping this photograph.

(*Below*)   Another photograph of class S15 30847 climbing Honiton Bank on 3 August 1955. This was the picture taken by John Robertson and shows Willie Hermiston taking the previous photograph. Although the coaches are numbered as a 3-set, the last coach does not appear to belong.

(Above)   Adams '0395' class 0-6-0 No 30564 makes an unusual pilot for Bulleid 'Battle of Britain' class 4-6-0 No 34061 '73 Squadron' on the head of the Atlantic Coast Express as it runs into Platform 3 at Exeter St Davids on 7 August 1954. 30564 had probably been shunting at Meldon Quarry and was returning to Exmouth Junction shed. The 0395 class were employed on ballasting and light branch work but also saw service in Palestine, Mesopotamia and Salonika during the 1914-18 war. Four of the locomotives sent to war were lost on the 'Arabic' when the ship was torpedoed in the Mediterranean.   *Photo: J Robertson.*

(Below)   Bulleid 'West Country' class 4-6-2 No 34004 'Yeovil' starts a Plymouth to Waterloo service away from Exeter St Davids on 31 July 1955.   *Photo: W Hermiston.*

(Left) Salisbury based 'H15' class 4-6-0 No 30335 takes the Salisbury line under Battledown Flyover with a Down working of empty ballast hoppers bound for Meldon Quarry on 16 May 1959. The locomotive was withdrawn one month after this picture was taken and scrapped at Eastleigh Works in September 1959. The class was a mixture of designs and rebuilds by Urie and Maunsell and were employed on all types of trains. The brake-van is fitted with a plough for use on permanent way trains to spread ballast; the angle of the scoop was adjusted by use of control-wheels. The down Bournemouth line can be seen to the right of the picture.

Photo: J Robertson.

(Below)   B4 class 0-4-0 No 30083 which was built at Nine Elms in 1908 and allocated to Plymouth to work the docks is seen at rest at Plymouth Friary in 1954. The spark arrester was to protect the wooden piers. The B4s were designed by Mr Adams for dock shunting; 14 were allocated to Southampton Docks, 4 to Plymouth Docks, 2 to Poole Harbour, and the remainder were based at Eastleigh. The damage to the brickwork above the window arches of the building behind the locomotive was the result of bomb damage.

Photo: W Hermiston.

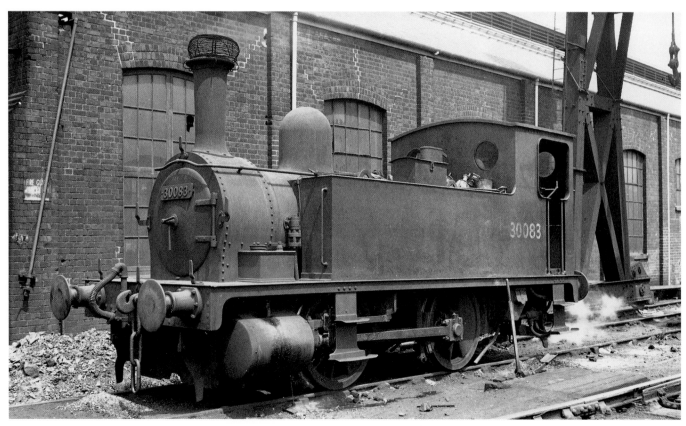

(*Above*)   Johnson 3F 0-6-0T No M7203, fitted with condensing, on shed at Cricklewood. The engine carries its new number denoting Midland section and was soon to become 47203. Although British Railways has been applied to the tank, the locomotive still carried its original LMS smokebox numberplate. Note the shunter's brake-stick laid on the footplate alongside the splasher. Cricklewood was equipped with an automatic coaling-plant which can be seen in the background.   *Photo: W Hermiston.*

(*Below*)   Hughes 'Crab' 5MT 4-6-0 No 42792 stands in front of the old brewery at Kentish Town in July 1953. The 'Crabs' were an instant success when introduced in 1927 and there was little that they could not tackle. By 1932, a total of 245 engines had entered service and Stanier used them as a basis for a new design and added another 40 to this total.   *Photo: W Hermiston.*

(Above) Ivatt 4MT 2-6-0 No 43022 in early British Railways' livery is pictured on Devon Road shed. These locomotives had extremely high running plates above the driving wheels earning them the nickname 'Flying Pigs'. They were primarily for use on local passenger and freight trains but could occasionally be seen on express workings and acting as pilots. 43022 was finally withdrawn from Stoke in December 1966.   *Photo: W Hermiston.*

(Below) 'Patriot' class 6P No 45501 'St. Dunstan's' at Camden on 19 May 1958. This engine was a 3-cylinder rebuild by Fowler of the old London and North Western 'Claughton' class, which was introduced in 1912, using the original wheels.   *Photo: J Robertson.*

(Above) Ivatt 2MT 2-6-2T No 41306 banks a train, headed by 'Battle of Britain' class No 34050 'Royal Observer Corps', out of Exeter St Davids for Exeter Central on 31 July 1955. These locomotives were found on all regions of British Railways and were used principally for branch line working as well as shed and station pilot duties.   *Photo: J Robertson.*

(Below) 8F 2-8-0 No 48410 heads a freight train out of Teignmouth on 2 August 1955. The 8F was a Stanier design and the locomotives became the workhorses of the London, Midland & Scottish Railway. They were ideal for heavy, long-distance freight workings but were also comfortable on passenger work. Many of the class saw war service overseas. 48410 was eventually transferred to Wigan and finally worked at Rose Grove until August 1968, the end of regular steam on British Railways.   *Photo: J Robertson.*

(*Left*) 'Patriot' 7P 4-6-0 No 45536 'Private W Wood VC' is seen at speed at Tring on 3 August 1957. 45536 was rebuilt in October 1948 with a 2A type taper boiler and reclassified 7P.

Photo: J Robertson.

50

(Above) 'Royal Scot' class 4-6-0 No 46128 'The Lovat Scouts', in early British Railways livery, hurries through Colwyn Bay. Introduced in 1943, the class were Stanier rebuilds of Fowler locomotives and fitted with taper boiler, new cylinders and double chimney. 46128 was later fitted with smoke deflectors. *Photo: W Hermiston.*

(Above) G2a class 7F 0-8-0 No 48945, possibly at Shrewsbury in the late 1940s. These locomotives never carried smokebox numberplates as the smokebox doors were too thin for the mountings. The G2a class were 1936 rebuilds of the ex-London North Western Railway G1 locomotives. 48945 was finally withdrawn in March 1959. *Photo: W Hermiston.*

(Left) Fowler 4MT 2-6-4T No 42415 has its tanks filled at Afon Wen on 10 July 1954. The 'gaffer' in the trilby hat is being unusually helpful by working the valve-release chain on the water column.

Photo: J Robertson.

(Below) Stanier 3MT 2-6-2T No 40102 takes water at Afon Wen on 10 July 1954. These engines were a development of the 1930 Fowler 2-6-2s with taper boilers and were never deemed to be good steamers. 40102 finally succumbed to the cutter's torch at Maden & McKee, Stanley, Liverpool in March 1962, having been in store at Birkenhead from withdrawal in October 1961. *Photo: J Robertson.*

(Above) Stanier 2-cylinder 4MT 2-6-4T No M2447 between duties at Crewe South on 7 August 1948. The 'M' preceding the locomotive's number signified the 'Midland Section' and was used before the decision was taken to renumber totally all locomotives.   *Photo: Anon.*

(Above) 'Royal Scot' class 4-6-0 No 46113 'Cameronian' is captured at Crewe North, sporting an unrebuilt parallel boiler and unshaded LMS lettering on the tender, in July 1949. 46113 made a world's record run by taking a train non-stop from Euston to Glasgow in April 1928, a distance of 401.5 miles.   *Photo: Anon.*

(*Above*) 'Patriot' class 6P No 45506 'The Royal Pioneer Corps' at rest on Crewe North shed on 8 August 1953. Nos 45502 to 45515. were new engines built to Fowler's design and introduced in 1933. Officially, this batch of locomotives was considered as rebuilds.
Photo: A G Ellis.

(*Above*) 'Princess Royal' class 4-6-0 No 46210 'Lady Patricia' shows off her elegant lines at Crewe on 25 July 1952. This pioneer class of LMS Pacifics could trace their 4-cylinder design background to the GWR 'Stars', 'Castles' and 'Kings'. This was hardly surprising as Stanier had worked at Swindon and must have been influenced by Dean and Churchward.
Photo: J Robertson.

(Above) Beyer-Garratt 2-6-6-2T No 47990 at York with an iron-ore train in June 1952. These locomotives were virtually two 2-6-0 engines mounted cab-to-cab. Normal engine boiler and cab, mounted centrally between rectangular tank at front end, and a 10-ton capacity round-topped revolving coal bunker at rear. The length of the locomotive was an astonishing 87ft and 10.5ins. The last of the class was withdrawn in April 1958. *Photo: Anon.*

(Below) 4F 0-6-0 No 44136 at rest at York. The 4F was a development of an earlier Midland Railway design and introduced in 1924. The locomotives were well suited to mineral workings and were known to railwaymen as 'Duck Sixes'. The class remained extant until 1959 when 44 locomotives were withdrawn, 44136 being one of them in December 1959 from Hasland. *Photo: W Hermiston.*

(Above) Hughes 6P5F 2-6-0 No 42900 speeds through York on 6 August 1953. At the time of this picture, 42900 was shedded at Saltley but finished her days at Stockport from where she was withdrawn from service in October 1965. *Photo: J Robertson.*

(Below) Ivatt 4MT 2-6-0 'Mogul' No 43134 stands with a mixed freight in an unknown goods yard. Built by British Railways in December 1951, 43134 was withdrawn only 15 years later from Ardsley in February 1965. The first withdrawals of the class did not occur until 1963 and 6 engines remained in service in 1968, the final being No 43106 which was withdrawn on 23 June 1968 and later preserved. *Photo: J Robertson.*

(Above) Ivatt 2MT 2-6-0 'Mogul' No 46472 waits to receive water at its home shed of Darlington on 1 August 1953. The engine was fitted with a self-cleaning smokebox as denoted by the 'SC' plate fitted to the shedcode. *Photo: J Robertson.*

(Above) Fowler 7F 0-8-0 No 49511 stands on her home shed at Wigan on 27 July 1952. This class of heavy freight locomotives was developed by Fowler from the old London and North Western G2 class and introduced in 1929. 49511 eventually transferred to Newton Heath where she remained until withdrawal in May 1959. *Photo: A G Ellis.*

(Above) 'Jubilee' class 4-6-0 No 45671 'Prince Rupert' departs from Carlisle with the Glasgow to Manchester train watched by 2-6-4T No 42544 on 20 August 1952. 45671 was a Newton Heath engine which was retained primarily to work this service. *Photo: J Robertson.*

(Above) 'Royal Scot' class 7P 4-6-0 No 46117 'Welsh Guardsman' at Carlisle on the Up 'The Thames-Clyde Express' on 23 August 1952. The train ran from St Pancras to Glasgow via Settle and Carlisle. Built in October 1927, 46117 was converted to a taper boiler (2A type) in December 1943 and finished her days at Leeds (Neville Hill) in 1963.

Photo: J Robertson.

(Above) 'Jubilee' class 4-6-0 No 45713 'Renown', fitted with Fowler tender and large St Rollox cabside number, poses with her crew at Kingmoor shed on 18 April 1955. Introduced in 1934, the 'Jubilee' class was a taper boiler version of the 'Patriot' class designed for express passenger trains. 45713 was built in July 1936 and finally withdrawn in October 1962. *Photo: J Robertson.*

(Above) 'Princess Royal' class 4-6-2 No 46212 'Duchess of Kent' heads 'The Mid-Day Scot' at Straw Frank, south of Carstairs on 21 July 1956. 46212 remained shedded at Crewe North until put into store at Crewe South from September 1961 to March 1962, before being scrapped at Crewe Works one month later. *Photo: J Robertson.*

(Left) 'Princess Coronation' class 4-6-0 No 46233 'Duchess of Sutherland' lifts a train up Beattock on 26 July 1952. 46233 was never streamlined and worked until 1964, the class' final year in service.
Photo: J Robertson.

(Right) 5F 4-6-0 No 44669 pilots 'Britannia' Pacific 7MT 4-6-2 No 70053 'Moray Firth' on Beattock on 16 July 1955. 70053 was built at Crewe in September 1954 and saw only 13 years' service, mostly on the Scottish Region.
Photo: J Robertson.

(Left) Midland Railway 4F 0-6-0 No 44326 stands at Beattock on a calm summer's day on 26 July 1952 with 'The Siege'. This train, comprising the coach in the picture, was provided for the railway colony that lived on Beattock Summit to gather supplies from the local town of Beattock. The coach was added to the back of a down freight and returned later on an up freight. *Photo: J Robertson.*

(Right) 'Princess Royal' class 4-6-2 No 46200 'The Princess Royal' heads up Beattock, near Harthope. John Robertson can be seen next to the telegraph pole in this picture taken by W Hermiston. When introduced in 1933, it was expected that the names of these locomotives would have a Scottish theme; however, an approach had been made covertly to the Monarch for permission to name the first locomotive after the Sovereign's daughter the Princess Royal. Once granted, Princess Royal became the class name and also the theme for naming subsequent engines after Royal ladies.

(Above) 'Princess Royal' class 4-6-2 No 46203 'Princess Margaret Rose' heads out of Carstairs on 17 June 1954. The class were the first locomotives to be built under the Stanier regime and the first 'Pacific' type to run on the London, Midland & Scottish Railway, used to haul major expresses on the West Coast Main line from Euston to Liverpool, Manchester and Glasgow. 46203 was finally saved for preservation by the Midland Steam Trust. *Photo: J Robertson.*

(Above) Ivatt 2MT 2-6-0 No 46461 is captured by the camera of John Robertson while traversing the Lauder Light Railway, 1 mile from Fountainhall, on 12 April 1952. The line closed to passenger traffic on 12 September 1932 and the former station yard at Lauder is now a small industrial estate.

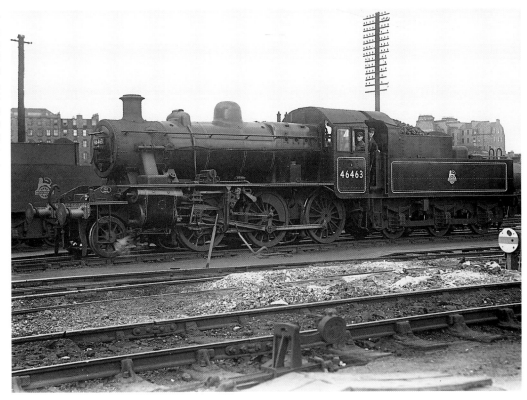

(Right) 'Mogul' Ivatt 4MT 2-6-0 No 46463 poses proudly with her crew at Dundee on 13 August 1950. The locomotive was only 2 months old when this picture was taken by John Robertson, having been constructed at Crewe in June 1950. The engine remained at Dundee during the whole of its short life, being withdrawn from there in February 1966. *Photo: J Robertson.*

(Above) 5F 4-6-0 No 44668 is turned at Haymarket shed on 17 July 1955. The 5Fs were colloquially known as 'Black Fives' from the combination of colour and power classification, but in the early years it was often called the 'Black Stanier' to distinguish it from the red 3-cylinder Jubilees.

Photo: J Robertson.

(*Above*) Hughes 6P5F 2-6-0 No 42737 at Parkhead on 25 April 1953. These locomotives were known as 'Crabs' and 42737 sports a smokebox numberplate edged in white which was a common practice on the Scottish Region. The engine was finally withdrawn from Ayr in December 1966. *Photo: J Robertson.*

(*Above*) 'Princess Coronation' class 4-6-2 No 46224 'Princess Alexandra' lifts 'The Royal Scot' away from Glasgow Central on 16 April 1955. The locomotive has a sloping smokebox as it was originally streamlined; the casing being removed in May 1946. *Photo J Robertson.*

(Left) 'Princess Royal' class 4-6-2 No 46201 'Princess Elizabeth' leaves Glasgow Central on 28 March 1959. 46201 was introduced in 1933 and was fitted with a Stanier taper boiler design. *Photo: J Robertson.*

(Above) 3-cylinder Compound 4P 4-4-0 No 40920 stands in Glasgow St Enoch station on 3 May 1952. The British Railways' number has been applied to the cabside by hand at St Rollox which always used larger numbers than other works. 40920 was built in July 1927 and withdrawn from Stranraer in May 1958. The 4Ps were a development of earlier Johnson Midland Railway compounds and were famous for their exploits on express workings. *Photo: Anon.*

(Above) Fowler 2F 0-6-0T No 47167 at Polmadie on 22 August 1953. In the picture, the engine carries no BR crest and the locomotive's number is applied to the tank as there was insufficient room on the bunker. 47167 was finally withdrawn from Greenock in July 1960.

Photo: J Robertson.

(Above) 'Princess Coronation' class 4-6-2 No 46220 'Coronation' on the down 'Royal Scot' at Motherwell on 6 June 1953. In the year of the Coronation of Queen Elizabeth II, the crest could be carried on named expresses; although the Midland Region enthused over the practice, the Western Region never indulged. 46220 was named 'Coronation' on the engine's completion in the summer of 1937, to honour the Coronation of King George VI.

Photo: J Robertson.

(*Above*) 'Jubilee' class 4-6-0 No 45645 'Collingwood' is ready for the road at Polmadie on 14 April 1956. Considered to be a poor engine, 45645 was built in December 1934 at a cost of £6,600 and was fitted with a cast nameplate with thin lettering.
Photo: J Robertson.

(*Above*)   McIntosh Caledonian '812' 0-6-0 No 57559 starts the 11.37am Glasgow stopper away from Edinburgh Princes Street on 21 April 1956. This design was introduced in 1899 and almost all of the 96 class members survived into British Railways' ownership.

Photo: J Robertson.

(*Below*)   LMS 4P 4-6-0 No 54634 is seen at Glasgow St Enoch on 3 May 1952. These engines were modified Caledonian '60' class and were known as 'Grey Backs' because they went as fast as a slug; in Scotland a slug was known as a 'Grey Back'.   *Photo: J Robertson.*

(Above) Highland Railway P 0-4-4T No 55051 at The Mound junction taking the dining-car off the train from Inverness in April 1951. The dining-car was used between Inverness and The Mound; passengers starting their journey from Wick or Thurso had to wait until arrival at The Mound before they could have breakfast. 55051 was one of 4 engines of the class designed by P Drummond and built in 1905. When not on dining-car duty, 55051 and 55053 worked the Dornoch branch and were the last Highland Railway engines to remain in ordinary service on British Railways.   *Photo: Anon.*

(Below) Caledonian 2P 0-4-4T No 55208 in early British Railways livery is seen on a Perth train leaving Ladybank on 13 May 1950. Incongruously, the engine has a North British chimney fitted which would almost certainly have been unpopular with ex-Caledonian railwaymen.   *Photo: J Robertson.*

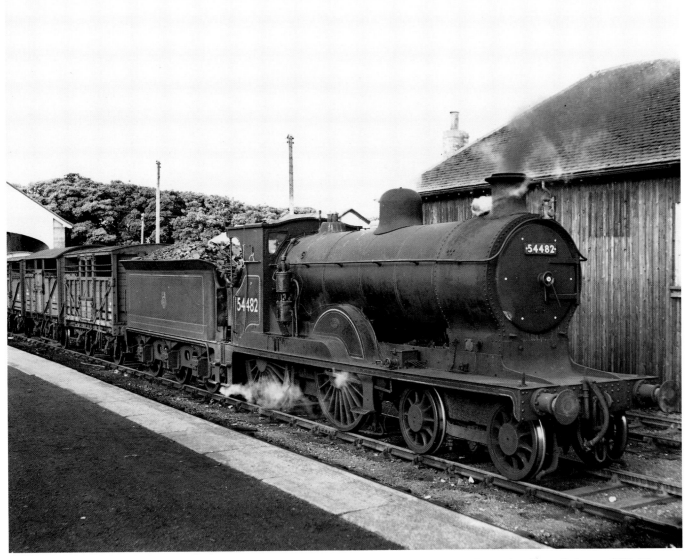

(Above) Pickersgill Caledonian '72' class 4-4-0 No 54482 waits for the road at Thurso with a livestock train on 19 August 1960. The crew member uses the time to catch up on some sleep. 54482 soldiered on at Aviemore until February 1962 when it was withdrawn and broken up at Arnott Young, West of Scotland Shipbreaking Company, Troon in November 1963.   *Photo: J Robertson.*

(Right) North London Railway 2F 0-6-0T No 58856 on the Stephenson Locomotive Society's High Peak Railtour at Finden on 25 April 1953. The passengers on this special stood in the open wagons for the trip over the High Peak line.   *Photo: Anon.*

(Left) Aspinall rebuilt (Lancashire & Yorkshire 23 class) 2F 0-6-0ST No 51419 at Fleetwood on 1 June 1957. Originally built 1876-87 as Barton Wright 0-6-0 tender engines, the class was rebuilt by Aspinall in 1891–1900 as saddle tanks. 51419 was used to shunt Goole docks and, despite her age, lasted until withdrawal in September 1961.

Photo: Anon.

(Right) A4 pacific 4-6-2 No 60004 'William Whitelaw', in British Railways' blue livery, makes a fine sight as she departs from Edinburgh Waverley with the 10.24am working on 24 March 1951.

Photo: J Robertson.

(Above) Lancashire & Yorkshire 3F 0-6-0 No 52338 had enjoyed better days at Cetane Oak before it was seen here on withdrawal at Horwich Works on 2 June 1957. The engine was broken up at the Works 2 months later.
Photo: A G Ellis.

(*Above*) Peppercorn A1 class 4-6-2 No 60142 'Edward Fletcher' leaves Edinburgh Waverley with the 10.0am 'The Flying Scotsman' service to Kings Cross on 24 March 1951. After a period of austerity when nameplates were not affixed to locomotives to save money, the A1s began to receive names from April 1950. 60142 was named at Newcastle Central station by the Lord Mayor on 30 October 1950. *Photo: J Robertson.*

(*Left*) Gresley D49/1 'Shire' class 4-4-0 No 62715 'Roxburghshire', fitted with GC tender approaches Edinburgh Waverley on the 11.45am Peebles to Edinburgh service on 24 March 1951. 62715 was built at Darlington in March 1928 and was withdrawn from service in June 1959.
Photo: J Robertson.

(Left) Thompson B1 class 4-6-0 No 61178 in early British Railways' livery bursts into the sunlight to pass through Princes Street Gardens having just departed from Edinburgh Waverley on 7 October 1950. At Haymarket shed 61178 and 61244 were allotted to regular men on a double-shift basis, and enthusiastic drivers made a special effort to maintain their engines in perfect external condition.

Photo: J Robertson.

(Above)   Gresley V2 2-6-2 No 60835 'The Green Howard, Alexandra, Princess of Wales's Own Yorkshire Regiment' passes Portobello West signal box at Haymarket West in May 1955. Fettes Public School can be seen in the background. 60835 was built at Darlington in 1938 and named at Richmond station on 24 September 1938 by Maj-Gen H E Franklyn, GOC Catterick Division and Colonel of the Regiment, to mark the 250th Anniversary of the raising of the Regiment (as Luttrell's Regiment, later the 19th Foot) in 1688.

Photo: W Hermiston.

(Above)   Gresley A4 class 4-6-2 No 60010 'Dominion of Canada' in blue livery at Longniddry in 1948. 60010 was fitted with a Canadian Pacific Railroad bell and whistle on 11 March 1938 which was a gift from that Company.   *Photo: J Robertson.*

(Above)   Gresley A3 class 4-6-2 No 60041 'Salmon Trout', in blue livery, heads 'The Queen of Scots' at Craigentinny on the frosty morning of 27 January 1951. The engine was named after a racehorse which won the 1924 St Leger and was owned by the Aga Khan.
Photo: J Robertson.

(Above)   A3 class 4-6-2 No 60087 'Blenheim' heads an express freight through North Queensferry on 18 September 1950. The locomotive was not named after the famous German bomber but the Aga Khan's racehorse which won The Derby in 1930.   *Photo: J Robertson.*

(Below)   A2 class 4-6-2 No 60529 'Pearl Diver' sweeps through North Queensferry on 18 September 1950. 60529 was rebuilt with double blast-pipe and Melesco multiple-valve regulator. The engine was transferred from Haymarket shed to St Margaret's in November 1961 and was withdrawn from service in October 1962.   *Photo: J Robertson.*

(Above) Class D11 4-4-0 No 62688 'Ellen Douglas', in apple-green, is seen at North Queensferry under a threatening sky on 18 September 1950. The class was built by Armstrong Whitworth & Company in November 1924 and named in October 1925 after characters in the novels and poems of Sir Walter Scott. Of course, 'Ellen Douglas' and 'The Lady of the Lake', the name applied to No 62690, were one and the same person.   *Photo: J Robertson.*

(Right) Gresley V3 class 2-6-2T No 67675 is viewed at Inverkeithing on 14 July 1951. Jamestown can be seen on the left of the picture and the line running under the main line was the branch to Rosyth Dockyard. The V3s were designed for mixed traffic and were used widely in the North East of England and in Scotland. All the Scottish allocated engines were condemned by January 1963, including 67675 which was withdrawn in December 1962 from Eastfield, Glasgow.

Photo: J Robertson.

(*Left*) D49 'Shire' 4-4-0 No 62711 'Dumbarton-shire' eases a freight past Saughton Junction on 1 June 1951. Saughton Junction lies just west of Hay-market where the Dundee line joins the line from the Forth Bridge.
Photo: J Robertson.

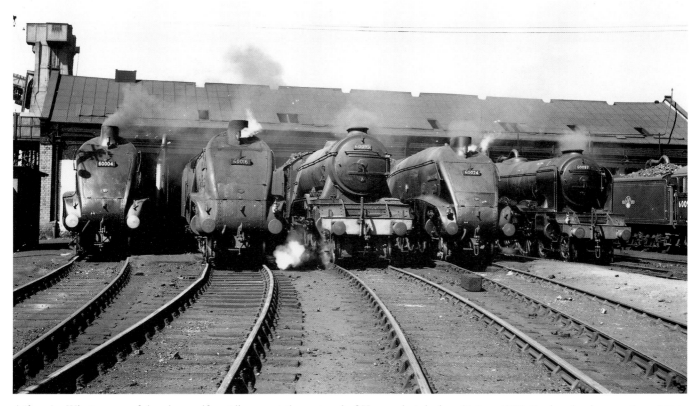

(Above)   What a powerful and magnificent line-up at the east end of Haymarket shed on 21 June 1959. Engines in view are, from left to right, A4 60004 'William Whitelaw', A4 60016 'Silver King', A3 60095 'Flamingo', A4 60024 'Kingfisher', A3 60097 'Humorist', and A3 60099 'Call Boy'.
Photo: J Robertson.

(Below)   Peppercorn A2 class 4-6-2 No 60530 'Sayajirao' poses on Haymarket Motive Power Depot with shed cleaners. The more mature gentleman to the left of the group was the 'Gaffer', a former driver who had been removed from the footplate on medical grounds. With the exception of the first of class, all engines carried names of famous racehorses. The horse Sayajirao was owned by Maharaja of Baroda and won the St Leger in 1947.
Photo: J Robertson.

(Above) A diversion from locomotives as the Motive Power Instruction Car (No 2A) is pictured at Haymarket shed on 30 September 1950. The coach would have been used for mutual improvements classes and general instruction. *Photo: J Robertson.*

(Below) 'Headboards at Haymarket' on 6 October 1957. What value would the railwayana market put on this collection today?
Photo: J Robertson.

(Above) Peppercorn A1 class 4-6-2 No 60138 'Boswell' shows off her powerful and elegant lines at Haymarket. These engines were distinguishable from the A3s by almost vertical ends to front ends of main-frame over front buffer-beam. The footplate was angled to clear the driving wheels, over which hardly any splashers were visible. 60138 was named after the racehorse which was owned by Mr W Woodward and won the 1936 St Leger.   *Photo: J Robertson.*

(Below) J69 class 0-6-0T No 68505 at South Leith on 5 April 1952. The new nationalised company was very economical with its paint, as is apparent with the original LNER lettering already showing through on the tank-side. The J69s were rebuilds of the J67s and were originally passenger locomotives for the London suburban area.   *Photo: J Robertson.*

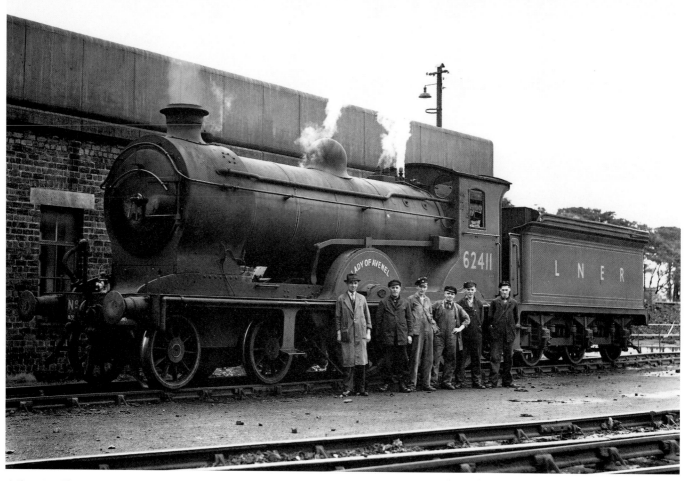

(Above) Class D29 4-4-0 No 62411 'Lady of Avenel' poses with shed staff at Polmont. The D29s were commonly known as the 'Scott' class because the engine names were associated with the literary works of Sir Walter Scott. 62411 was the only member of the class to carry lined-green livery, lettered LNER, into British Railways' service. *Photo: J Robertson.*

(Below) Class D33 4-4-0 No 62457 stands elegantly on the turntable at Eastfield on 11 April 1949. Out of a total of 12 for the class, 10 survived to come into British Railways' ownership. The engines were a mixed-traffic version of the original 'Scott' class of 1909 (LNER class D29). 62457 was built at Cowlairs in November 1909 and was withdrawn in June 1952. *Photo: J Robertson.*

(Above) Gresley K2/2 2-6-0 No 61781 'Loch Morar' pilots 'Black Five' No 45136 up the Cowlair's incline on 23 September 1950. The incline was originally worked by ropes. The picture shows clearly the sordidness of Glasgow at that time with its municipal-bound factories.   *Photo: J Robertson.*

(Right) Holden J67/1 class 0-6-0T No 68511 at Galashiels on 10 July 1950. The engine was used on the Lauder Light Railway and to reduce axle loadings, because of the light weight track of the branch, the engine ran with empty tanks and carried water in the attached tender.

Photo: A G Ellis.

(Above) Gresley A4 4-6-2 No 60004 'William Whitelaw' heads 'The Queen of Scots' at Ayton on 3 June 1950. On 2 March 1962, 60004 took over 'The Aberdeen Flyer' from 60022 'Mallard' at Edinburgh. This train was a special that was to have been the last non-stop run of all between London and Edinburgh. In the event 'Mallard' was stopped at Chathill because of a hot box on a preceding freight.

Photo: J Robertson.

(Left) Gresley V2 class 2-6-2 No 60868 at Lady Victoria in September 1948. The V2s numbered 184, the most famous of which was 60800 'Green Arrow'. Generally used as mixed traffic locomotives, they were originally introduced for working fast freights.

Photo: J Robertson.

(Above) K3/2 class 2-6-0 No 61968 runs along the coast at Burnmouth in the late afternoon sunshine on 2 July 1955. Introduced in 1924, the K3/2 class was a development of Gresley Great Northern design, built to London and North Eastern Railway loading-gauge.

Photo: J Robertson.

(Right) Peppercorn A1 class 4-6-2 No 60137 'Redgauntlet' on the CTAC express at Burnmouth on 2 July 1955. These handsome locomotives shared the major duties on the East Coast main line along with the A4s, A3s and A2s. 60137 was an early victim of withdrawal being taken out of service in October 1962.

Photo: J Robertson.

(*Left*) **B12/1** class 4-6-0 No 61501 backs into the shed at Kittybrewster in 1949. 61501 was built at Stratford in February 1912, transferred to Scotland in July 1931 and was withdrawn from service in May 1953. Though nominally the design of Holden, these B12s were purely the work of the Stratford Drawing Office.

Photo: J Robertson.

90

(Above) Gresley B12 class 4-6-0 No 61560 is prepared for the road at Kittybrewster in 1949. The engine sports LNER apple-green livery with British Railways' unshaded lettering on the tender. The apple-green was applied directly over the original LNER pre-war paint.

Photo: J Robertson.

(Above) Wordswell F4 class 2-4-2T No 67157 approaches the turntable at Fraserburgh on 30 August 1952. A total of 118 F4s were constructed between 1884 and 1909 but 67157 remained in service until June 1956 to work the St Coombs Light Railway, hence the cow-catcher, and was the last survivor of the class. The line from Dyce Junction to Fraserburgh closed on 4 October 1965 having been preceded by the St Coombs branch 5 months earlier.

Photo: J Robertson.

(*Above*) This photograph of Pickersgill's Great North of Scotland design class D40 4-4-0 No 62264 at Keith in 1955, is the only picture of his work that hangs in John Robertson's retirement flat in Leith, Edinburgh; therefore, I believe it is only right that it should be included in this book of his work.

(Above) Gresley A4 pacific 4-6-2 No 60034 'Lord Faringdon', fitted with Kylchap blast pipe and double chimney, has a clear road through Selby, the home of the Headquarters of the British Oil and Cake Mills. *Photo: J Robertson.*

(Below) Wordsell G5 class 0-4-4T No 67340 probably at Hull Botanic Gardens. 67340 was the only engine in the class of 110 to have extended side tanks; it was also fitted with push-pull gear, along with 17 others. Built at Darlington in September 1901, 67340 was withdrawn from service in April 1958. *Photo: W Hermiston.*

(*Left*) Gresley A8 class 4-6-2T No 69860 lays a smoke-screen over Whitby as it departs with a scenic excursion on 2 August 1953. These engines were rebuilt by Gresley in 1931 from the old North Eastern 'D' class of 4-4-4T type and usually worked in old North Eastern Railway areas.

Photo: J Robertson.

(Above) Thompson B1 class 4-6-0 No 61020 'Gemsbok', a visitor from Low Moor, is seen at Darlington on 20 April 1959. Only 49 out of the 410 engines in the class were named and of these, 40 were 'antelope' names, a further 18 were names of LNER directors and the odd one was 'Mayflower', the only name allotted after nationalisation.   *Photo: J Robertson.*

(Right) Great Eastern signals are much in evidence in this picture of J20/1 0-6-0 No 64695 at March on 13 August 1954. The class was designed by Hill and introduced in 1943 primarily for freight workings. Although 64695 escaped the first withdrawals in 1959, she only remained in service until January 1960 and was broken up at Stratford a month later.

Photo: J Robertson.

(Above) D16/3 class 4-4-0 No 62596 at Norwich on 8 August 1953. Introduced in 1938, the D16/3 was a rebuild of the D16/2 with round-topped boiler, but retaining original footplating and slide valves. 62596 remained at Norwich until withdrawal in October 1957.

Photo: J Robertson.

(Below) During his holiday to the East of England in 1953, John Robertson photographed Thompson L1 class 2-6-4T No 67708 drifting into Ipswich on 10 August 1953 with a mixed rake of Gresley and Thompson coaches and a Great Central van, probably bound for Stratford Works. These engines were introduced in 1945 and were used on heavy suburban passenger trains and, occasionally, on express workings. 67708 was withdrawn from service in December 1960 and the remaining 65 engines fell victim to the mass withdrawals of 1962 and the class was extinct by the end of that year. Worthy of note is the mix of modem colour-light signalling and antiquated gas-lighting on the platforms.

(Above) Class F6 2-4-2T No 67231 is seen on station pilot duties at Lowestoft on 9 August 1953. The F6s were known as 'Gobblers' by their crews because of the large quantities of coal that the engines consumed. *Photo: J Robertson.*

(Below) B17/4 class 4-6-0 No 61648 'Arsenal' is made ready for her next duty at Stratford on 19 December 1957. On one occasion, 61648 was recorded having run the 103.1 miles from Leicester to Marylebone with a gross load of 465 tons (thirteen bogies) in 110 minutes and 6 seconds which included a permanent way check. *Photo: J Robertson.*

(Left) Britannia Pacific 4-6-2 No 70004 'William Shakespeare' is readied at Dover on 8 August 1956 to take the Up 'Golden Arrow' to Victoria. 70004 was treated to a special finish for display at the Festival of Britain Exhibition in 1951. The locomotive was maintained in superb condition by Stewarts Lane shed, until transferred to Kentish Town in June 1958.

Photo: J Robertson.

(Above) On the same day No 70004 'William Shakespeare' leaves Dover on the 'Golden Arrow'. 70004 continued in service until January 1968, being withdrawn from Carlisle (Kingmoor) and scrapped by Wards of Inverkeithing in April 1968. The most serious of the teething troubles experienced with the class was wheels shifting on axles; one of the first instances of the problem was noted when 70004 was at speed near Headcorn on the 'Golden Arrow'.

Photo: J Robertson.

(Above) Britannia Pacific 7MT 4-6-2 No 70040 'Clive of India' crosses Trowse swing bridge on 13 August 1953. Trowse swing bridge was situated between Trowse and Whitlingham on the former Great Eastern line from Thetford to Yarmouth. The naming of the class did not follow any particular theme, with the exception of the locomotives allocated to the Western and Scottish Regions. The Western Region engines were given names originally carried by GWR locomotives, and the Scottish Britannias bore the names of some of the Scottish firths.   *Photo: J Robertson.*

(Below) Britannia Pacific 4-6-2 No 70009 'Alfred the Great' at Norwich on 13 August 1953. All of the class were built at Crewe and 70009 was completed in May 1951 and withdrawn from Carlisle (Kingmoor) in January 1967.   *Photo: J Robertson.*

(Above) Western Region Britannia 4-6-2 No 70029 'Shooting Star' receives many admiring glances from 'the pack' at Swindon as it heads the Up 'Red Dragon' on 10 August 1955. 70029 was named after the Churchward 'Star' class 4-6-0 No 4009 which was withdrawn in March 1951. *Photo J Robertson.*

(Above) Scottish Region Britannia 4-6-2 No 70051 'Firth of Forth' leaves Edinburgh Princes Street on 11.47am stopping service to Glasgow on 21 April 1956 with non-corridor stock and watched by Fairburn 2-6-4T No 42273. The engine sports a Caley route indicator which showed signalmen where the train was bound. One of the nameplates off the locomotive sold at Sheffield Railwayana Auction in March 1997 for £10,300. Edinburgh Princes Street station closed to traffic on 6 September 1965. *Photo: J Robertson.*

(*Above*) Class 8P 4-6-2 No 71000 'Duke of Gloucester' resplendent with 'The Mid-Day Scot' headboard at Polmadie shed on 25 September 1954. This photograph was taken 5 months after the engine was constructed at Crewe to replace the Stanier Pacific 46202 destroyed in the Harrow disaster 2 years earlier. From July 1954, 'The Mid-Day Scot' was the first regular working for this engine following its return to Crewe after being on display at the International Railway Congress exhibition at Willesden during May 1954. The locomotive was sold in November 1967, and taken to Woodham Brothers site at Barry, South Wales, from where it was purchased in 1973 by the Duke of Gloucester Steam Locomotive Trust and returned to working order. *Photo: J Robertson.*

(*Above*)   Clan Pacific 6MT 4-6-2 No 72003 'Clan Fraser' at Symington on 19 April 1952. The class was introduced in 1952 and all ten members were allocated to the Scottish Region. The second batch of 'Clans' was never built as they were deemed unnecessary because of the already successful performance of the Class 5 4-6-0s. *Photo: J Robertson.*

(Above) Clan Pacific 4-6-2 No 72009 'Clan Stewart' climbs Beattock on 22 August 1952 with a Glasgow to Manchester train; when this picture was taken the engine was only 5 months old. 72009 was withdrawn from service in August 1965 from Carlisle (Kingmoor) and was only outlived by 2 other members of the class: 72007 'Clan MacKintosh', December 1965; and 72008 'Clan MacLeod', April 1966.

Photo: J Robertson.

(Below) Standard Class 5 4-6-0 No 73109 stands at Perth. The Standard Class 5s were numbered from 73000, designed at Doncaster, and first built in 1951. 73109 was constructed at Doncaster in 1955 and operated on the Scottish Region. The engine was withdrawn from service in October 1964 from Eastfield (Glasgow) at the ripe old age of 9!

Photo: J Robertson.

(Above) Standard Class 5 No 73143 heads a train through Melton Mowbray in 1960. 73143 almost lasted until the end of steam but was withdrawn from Patricroft in June 1968.

Photo: Anon.

(Below) Standard Class 4 4-6-0 No 75077 at Folkestone on 14 August 1956. The Class 4s fulfilled the requirement for a tender locomotive design which could provide a larger working range than a tank engine for use on routes such as in Central Wales. It was developed from the London Midland Region Class 4 2-6-4T design, which already had a good reputation for performance. 75077 spent her 12-year life on the Southern Region being withdrawn at the end of steam on that Region in July 1967.

Photo: J Robertson.

(Above) Doncaster built Standard Class 4MT 2-6-0 No 76061 is brand new in this picture taken at Brighton on 31 July 1955. The class was constructed at Doncaster, Derby and Horwich between December 1952 and October 1957 and the minimum repair period was an impressive 30 months. *Photo: J Robertson.*

(Below) Standard Class 3 2-6-0 No 77006 pictured at Glasgow Central in July 1954. Although a Scottish Region engine, 77006 was built at Swindon in 1953. The class was originally intended for mixed-traffic for use on the small number of lines where the Class 4 2-6-0s were excluded for reasons of weight. *Photo: C L Kerr.*

(*Above*) Standard Class 2 2-6-0 No 78048 at St Margaret's shed, Edinburgh on 11 March 1956. The Class 2s were the smallest of the Standard 2-6-0s and first appeared in 1953. The engines were used on freight and light main line and cross-country passenger workings; on the Western Region they were adopted as replacements for various 0-6-0 classes. *Photo: J Robertson.*

(*Below*) Standard Class 4 2-6-4T No 80001 at Polmadie on 12 September 1953. The Standard tanks were based on the successful tank engines designed by Fairburn and Ivatt. 80001 was constructed a year earlier at Derby and withdrawn in July 1966 to be broken up by Metal Industries of Faslane. *Photo: J Robertson.*

(Above) Standard Class 4 2-6-4T No 80122 is brand new when seen here at Keith with a mixed train of LNER and LMS stock on 17 September 1955. 80122 was built at Brighton and the curve of the tanks was constructed to match the line of Bulleid stock.

Photo: J Robertson.

(Below) Standard Class 3 2-6-2T No 82016 at Eastleigh. The Class 3s were intended for use on suburban, cross-country and stopping passenger, and short-haul freight workings. Construction of the Class 2s was carried out at Crewe and Darlington. *Photo: W Hermiston.*

(Above) Class O7 2-8-0 No 63106 with a coal train at Ayton on 16 September 1950. Class O7s were introduced in 1943 as War Department locomotives and taken into LNER stock in 1946. 63106 was built by the North British Locomotive Company in October 1943 as Works No 4928, taken into running stock in January 1947 and numbered LNER No 3106 in March 1947. The engine received its first BR no 63106 in October 1948 and was subsequently renumbered as 90427 in December 1950. The locomotive was eventually withdrawn in June 1967 from Goole and scrapped at Drapers of Hull in January 1968.   *Photo: J T Robertson.*

(Above) Riddles 'Austerity' WD class 2-8-0 No 90690 heads a mixed freight near Grantshouse during the late afternoon of 4 July 1953. This photograph was taken prior to the application of a BR smokebox numberplate. Grantshouse is situated on the East Coast Main Line between Berwick and Edinburgh and was a favourite haunt of John Robertson. The new bridges in the picture were constructed after the flood of 1948.

Photo: J Robertson.

(Above) Standard class 9F 2-10-0 No 92098 on the turntable at Haymarket after casual repairs at Cowlairs. The 251 locomotives constructed to this design were the most numerous of the Standards. 92098 was fitted with air pumps to work the Tyne-Dock to Consett iron-ore services. The engine was constructed at Crewe in July 1956 and served exactly 10 years, being withdrawn in July 1966 from Tyne Dock. *Photo: W Hermiston.*

(Above) 1Co-Co1 Nos 10201 and 10202 head 'The Royal Scot' at Glasgow Central on 6 April 1957. The locomotives were built at Ashford Works and were powered by English Electric Co 16-cylinder 1,750 bhp engines. *Photograph: J Robertson.*

(Above)   A1A-A1A Gas Turbine No 18000 inside Swindon Works where it seemed to spend most of its days. The locomotive was built in 1949 by the Swiss Locomotive & Machine works, Winter-thur and was powered by a Brown-Boveri 2,500 bhp Gas Turbine engine.

Photograph: Anon.

(Above)   Bo-Bo class EM1 1,500V DC overhead locomotive No 26019 at Mottram Yard. The locomotive was built at Doncaster in 1950 and equipped with four 467 hp Metropolitan-Vickers nose-suspended traction motors giving a maximum tractive effort of 45,000lb.

Photo: Anon.

(Above) A rare picture of Bo-Bo class ESI No 26500 in plain black at Heaton on 14 April 1957 before it was repainted in North Eastern green. The locomotive was introduced in 1902 and built by Brush Traction. It was powered by four BTH nose-suspended traction motors, using 630V DC overhead and 3rd rail, which produced a maximum tractive effort of 25,000lb.   *Photo: J Robertson.*

(Below) Co-Co 'Deltic' at Crewe on 3 June 1957. British Railways were providing facilities for road tests of this locomotive, which remained the property of English Electric. An order for 22 of these locomotives was eventually placed to work on the East, North-East and Scottish Regions.   *Photo: J Robertson.*

(Above) Bo-Bo Type 2 No D5322 at Leith Central on 10 May 1959. The engine was built by Birmingham R.C. & W. Company in 1958 and was fitted with a Sulzer 6-cylinder YLDA28 which produced 1,160 bhp at 750 rpm. Leith Central was closed to passenger traffic on 7 April 1952 and later opened for a short period as a diesel servicing depot. John Robertson's retirement flat now stands on the old trackbed which once led to Leith Central.   *Photo: J Robertson.*

(Below) The sign of things to come as diesel multiple-unit 'Melbourne' is pictured at Cambridge on 1 April 1954. No 'April Fool' this, because in just 14 years, these units together with diesel and electric locomotives had completely eradicated John Robertson and friends' beloved steam locomotives from British Railways.   *Photo: J Robertson.*